THE *Skinny*
NUTRiBULLET
SLIMMING SMOOTHIES
RECIPE BOOK

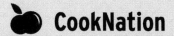 CookNation

THE SKINNY NUTRIBULLET SLIMMING SMOOTHIES RECIPE BOOK
DELICIOUS & NUTRITIOUS CALORIE COUNTED SMOOTHIES TO HELP YOU LOSE WEIGHT & FEEL GREAT!

ISBN 978-1-910771-68-6

A CIP catalogue record of this book is available from the British Library

• •

DISCLAIMER

This book is designed to provide information on smoothies and juices that can be made in the NUTRiBULLET appliance only, results may differ if alternative devices are used.

The NutriBullet™ is a registered trademark of Homeland Housewares, LLC. Bell & Mackenzie Publishing is not affiliated with the owner of the trademark and is not an authorized distributor of the trademark owner's products or services.
This publication has not been prepared, approved, or licensed by NutriBullet ™ or Homeland Housewares, LLC.

Some recipes may contain nuts or traces of nuts. Those suffering from any allergies associated with nuts should avoid any recipes containing nuts or nut based oils.
This information is provided and sold with the knowledge that the publisher and author do not offer any legal or other professional advice.
In the case of a need for any such expertise consult with the appropriate professional.
This book does not contain all information available on the subject, and other sources of recipes are available.
This book has not been created to be specific to any individual's or NUTRiBULLET's requirements.
Every effort has been made to make this book as accurate as possible. However, there may be typographical and or content errors. Therefore, this book should serve only as a general guide and not as the ultimate source of subject information.

This book contains information that might be dated and is intended only to educate and entertain.

The author and publisher shall have no liability or responsibility to any person or entity regarding any loss or damage incurred, or alleged to have incurred, directly or indirectly, by the information contained in this book.

CONTENTS

SUPERFOOD SMOOTHIES

VEGETABLE SMOOTHIES

NATURALLY SWEET SMOOTHIES   77

OTHER COOKNATION TITLES   95

INTRODUCTION

As well as tasting great smoothies are a powerful tool for aiding weight loss.

SMOOTHIES FOR WEIGHT LOSS

Using the NUTRiBULLET is a great way to aid a diet or weight management program. Our delicious recipes are packed with healthy ingredients, which will help you achieve your recommended daily quota of fruit and veg, yet are light on calories making them perfect for any diet plan.

All the recipes in this book are calorie counted to make sure you can keep an eye on your calorie intake. Replacing just one meal a day with one of our weight loss recipes will leave you feeling satisfied, knowing that the goodness in a glass is packed with nutrient dense ingredients. By stripping your diet of unhealthy processed foods weight loss becomes effortless and within days you'll feel brighter, stronger, more energetic and focussed.

The Skinny NUTRiBULLET Slimming Smoothies Recipe Book is packed with delicious and simple recipes. Benefits can include weight loss, rejuvenation, glowing skin, increased energy, lower blood pressure, lower cholesterol and overall enhanced wellbeing.

All our recipes make use of the tall cup of the NUTRiBULLET and the extractor blade. Feel free to experiment. Mixing your ingredients is fun and will help your create wonderful new combinations too. As a basic formula work on 50% leafy greens 50% fruit, ¼ cup of seeds/nuts and water.

START RIGHT NOW

There has never been a better time to introduce health-boosting, weight reducing, wellbeing smoothies to your life. With a spiralling obesity epidemic in the western world which in turn is linked to a growing list of debilitating diseases and ailments including diabetes, high blood pressure, heart disease, high cholesterol, infertility, skin conditions and more, the future for many of us can look bleak. Combine this with the super-fast pace of modern life and we can be left feeling fatigued and lethargic, worsened by daily consumption of unhealthy foods.

If you are reading this you will likely already have purchased a NUTRiBULLET or perhaps are considering buying one. A smart choice! The NUTRiBULLET is unquestionably one of the highest performing smoothie creators on the market. Its clean lines and compact design look great in any kitchen. It's simple to use, easy to clean and the results are amazing.

You may have watched or read some of the NUTRiBULLET marketing videos and literature which make claims of using the power of the NUTRiBULLET to help you lose weight, boost your immune system and fight a number of ailments and diseases. Of course the 'healing' power comes from the foods we use to make our smoothies but the real difference with the NUTRiBULLET is that it EXTRACTS all the goodness of the ingredients. Unlike many juicers and blenders, which leave behind valuable fibre, the NUTRiBULLET pulverizes the food, breaking down their cell walls and unlocking the valuable nutrients so your body can absorb and use them.

You may have made your own smoothies in the past using a blender – you'll know even with a powerful device that there are often indigestible pieces of food left in your glass – not so with the NUTRiBULLET which uses 600 watts to breakdown every part of the food. The manufacturer calls it 'cyclonic action' running at 10,000 revolutions per minute but whatever the marketing jargon, the results speak for themselves.

The NUTRiBULLET is not a blender and not a juicer. It is a nutrient extractor, getting the very best from every ingredient you put in and delivering a nutrient packed smoothie. Nutriblast. Using the power of the NUTRiBULLET is an incredibly fast and efficient way of giving our bodies the goodness they need. Making the most of anti-oxidants to protect your cells, omega 3 fatty acids to help your joints, fibre to aid digestion and protein to build and repair muscles.

Just one nutrient packed Nutriblast a day can make a difference to the way you feel and it only takes seconds to make!

TIPS

To help make your Nutriblast fuss-free, follow these quick tips.

- Prepare your shopping list. Take some time to select which Nutriblasts you want to prepare in advance. As with all food shopping, make a note of all the ingredients and quantities you need. Depending on the ingredients it's best not to shop too far in advance to ensure you are getting the freshest produce available. We recommend buying organic produce whenever you can if your budget allows. Organic produce can give a better yield and flavour to your Nutriblast. Remember almost all fruit is fine to freeze too.
- Wash your fruit and veg before juicing. This needn't take up much time but all produce should be washed clean of any traces of bacteria, pesticides and insects.
- To save time prepare produce the night before for early morning Nutriblasts.
- Cut up any produce that may not fit into the tall cup, but only do this just before juicing to keep it as fresh as possible.
- Wash your Nutriblast parts immediately after juicing. As tempting as it may be to leave it till a little later you'll be glad you took the few minutes to rinse and wash before any residue has hardened.
- Substitute where you need to. If you can't source a particular ingredient, try another instead. More often than not you will find the use of a different fruit or veg makes a really interesting and delicious alternative. In our recipes we offer some advice on alternatives but have the confidence to make your own too!
- Some Nutriblasts are sweeter than others and it's a fact that some of the leafy green drinks can take a little getting used to. Try drinking these with a straw, you'll find them easier to drink and enjoy.
- Drink lots of water!

IMPORTANT – WHAT NOT TO USE IN YOUR NUTRIBLASTS

The manufacturers of NUTRiBULLET are very clear on the following warning. While the joy of making Nutriblasts is using whole fruit and vegetables there are a few seeds and pits which should be removed. The following contain chemicals which can release cyanide into the body when ingested so do not use any of the following in your Nutriblasts:

- Apple Seeds
- Cherry Pits
- Peach pits
- Apricot Pits
- Plum Pits

CLEANING

Cleaning the NUTRiBULLET is thankfully very easy. The manufacturer gives clear guidelines on how best to do this but here's a recap:

Make sure the NUTRiBULLET is unplugged before disassembling or cleaning.
Set aside the power base and blade holders as these should not be used in a dishwasher.
Use hot soapy water to clean the blades but do not immerse in boiling water as this can warp the plastic.

Use a damp cloth to clean the power base.
All cups and lids can be placed in a dishwasher.
For stubborn marks inside the cup, fill the cup 2/3 full of warm soapy water and screw on the milling blade. Attached to the power base and run for 20-30 seconds.

WARNING:

Do not put your hands or any utensils near the moving blade. Always ensure the NUTRiBULLET is unplugged when assembling/disassembling or cleaning.

ABOUT COOKNATION

CookNation is the leading publisher of innovative and practical recipe books for the modern, health conscious cook.

CookNation titles bring together delicious, easy and practical recipes with their unique approach - easy and delicious, no-nonsense recipes - making cooking for diets and healthy eating fast, simple and fun.

With a range of #1 best-selling titles - from the innovative 'Skinny' calorie-counted series, to the 5:2 Diet Recipes collection - CookNation recipe books prove that 'Diet' can still mean 'Delicious'!

Turn to the end of this book to browse all CookNation's recipe books

 CookNation

Skinny

NUTRiBULLET

CLEANSING SMOOTHIES

SPINACH, PINEAPPLE & AVOCADO SMOOTHIE

297 calories

Ingredients

ISOTONIC

- 300g/11oz spinach
- 250ml/8½floz coconut water
- 200g/7oz pineapple
- 40g/1½oz avocado
- Water

Method

1 Rinse the spinach well.

2 Peel the pineapple and cut into chunks. Peel and stone the avocado.

3 Add all the ingredients to the NUTRiBULLET tall cup. Make sure they do not go past the MAX line on your machine.

4 Add a little water if needed to take it up to the MAX line.

5 Twist on the NUTRiBULLET blade and blend until smooth.

CHEF'S NOTE
Avocados have plenty of vitamin E, A and zinc - all good for cleansing the skin.

APPLE, KALE & CELERY CLEANSE

250 calories

Ingredients

- 100g/3½oz apple
- 2 tbsp lemon juice
- 225g/8oz kale
- 1 stalk celery
- 1 tbsp fresh flat leaf parsley
- 1 tbsp flax seeds
- ¼ tsp ground cinnamon
- Water

Method

1 Rinse the apple, kale, celery and parsley. Cut any thick green stalks off the kale.

2 Core the apple but don't peel it.

3 Add all the ingredients to the NUTRiBULLET tall cup, finishing with the water. Make sure not to go past the MAX line on your machine.

4 Twist on the NUTRiBULLET blade and blend until smooth.

CHEF'S NOTE
Celery is believed to cleanse the blood.

TROPICAL SPICE CLEANSE

348 calories

Ingredients

- 75g/3oz kale
- 250ml/8½floz light coconut milk
- 200g/7oz pineapple
- 50g/2oz mango

- 1 tbsp lemon juice
- ½ tbsp fresh grated ginger
- ¼ tsp ground turmeric

Method

1 Rinse the kale well and cut off any thick green stalks.

2 Peel the pineapple and the mango. De-stone the mango.

3 Add everything to the NUTRiBULLET tall cup. Make sure the ingredients do not go past the MAX line on your machine.

4 Add a little water if needed to take it up to the MAX line.

5 Twist on the NUTRiBULLET blade and blend until smooth.

CHEF'S NOTE

Ginger helps digestion and has many anti-inflammatory and antioxidant qualities.

GREEN CLEANSING SMOOTHIE

158 calories

Ingredients

- 2 celery stalks
- 300g/11oz cucumber
- 125g/4oz kale
- 225g/8oz spinach

- 1 tbsp fresh coriander
- 1 lemon
- 100g/3½oz apple
- Water

Method

1 Rinse the ingredients well.

2 Cut any thick green stalks off the kale. Core the apple.

3 Peel and de-seed the lemon.

4 Add everything to the NUTRiBULLET tall cup. Finish with water, and ice if desired, making sure not to go past the MAX line on your machine.

5 Twist on the NUTRiBULLET blade and blend until smooth.

CHEF'S NOTE

Apples have long been used in traditional remedies for skin problems & anaemia.

BEETROOT BLAST

116 calories

Ingredients

VITAMIN K ➤

- 40g/1½oz beetroot leaves
- 150g/5oz orange
- 75g/3oz raw beetroot
- 1 tbsp lemon
- Water

Method

1 Rinse the leaves and place in the NUTRiBULLET tall cup.

2 Peel & de-seed the orange, break into rough segments and add to the cup.

3 Peel and dice the beetroot and add it, along with the lemon juice.

4 Add water to taste, making sure the ingredients do not go past the MAX line on your machine.

5 Twist on the NUTRiBULLET blade and blend until smooth.

CHEF'S NOTE
Beetroot flushes out the liver and citrus fruits are also natural detoxifiers.

PEAR & BANANA SMOOTHIE

250 calories

Ingredients

PROTEIN RICH

- 100g/3½oz pear
- 1 small banana
- 100ml/3½floz soya milk
- 2 tbsp natural low-fat yoghurt
- 2 tsp flax seeds

Method

1 Rinse and core the pear.

2 Peel the banana and break into three. Place them in the NUTRiBULLET tall cup.

3 Add the milk, yoghurt and flax seeds. Make sure the ingredients do not go past the MAX line on your machine.

4 Twist on the NUTRiBULLET blade and blend until smooth.

CHEF'S NOTE
Pears contain pectin that has a positive mild laxative effect on the body.

BERRY & BANANA SMOOTHIE

372 calories

Ingredients

- 150g/5oz strawberries
- 75g/3oz raspberries
- 1 small banana

- 200ml/7floz pomegranate juice
- 2 tbsp low fat yogurt
- Water

Method

1 Wash the berries and remove the green tops from the strawberries.

2 Peel the banana and break into three pieces.

3 Add the fruit to the NUTRiBULLET tall cup, along with the pomegranate juice and yoghurt. Make sure the ingredients do not go past the MAX line on your machine.

4 Add a little water or more juice if you want to take it up to the MAX line.

5 Twist on the NUTRiBULLET blade and blend until smooth.

CHEF'S NOTE
Strawberries are rich in vitamin C and potassium which help cleanse toxins from the body.

SPICED ORANGE & MANGO SMOOTHIE

159 calories

Ingredients

- 100g/3 ½oz orange
- 2cm/1 inch fresh root ginger
- 2 tbsp natural low-fat yogurt
- 75g/3oz mango
- ½ tbsp porridge oats
- 1 tsp ground cinnamon
- Water

Method

1 Peel and de-seed the orange.

2 Peel and de-stone the mango.

3 Grate the root ginger.

4 Add all the ingredients to the NUTRiBULLET tall cup, finishing with water to taste. Make sure the ingredients do not go past the MAX line on your machine.

5 Twist on the NUTRiBULLET blade and blend until smooth.

CHEF'S NOTE

Mango is bursting with nutrients that strengthen the immune system and promote weight loss. It also cleanses and rejuvenates the skin.

KIWI & BLUEBERRY SMOOTHIE

147 calories

Ingredients

LOWERS CHOLESTEROL

- 1 kiwi fruit
- 75g/3oz blueberries
- 2 tbsp low fat natural yogurt
- 1 tsp honey
- Water

Method

1 Rinse the blueberries.

2 Peel the kiwi fruit, cut it in half and add to the tall cup. Add the yoghurt, blueberries and honey.

3 Make sure the ingredients do not go past the MAX line on your machine.

4 Add a little water if needed to take it up to the MAX line.

5 Twist on the NUTRiBULLET blade and blend until smooth.

CHEF'S NOTE
Kiwi fruits are packed with vitamins A and E which help prevent free radicals as well as certain types of cancer. Kiwis also helps flush out toxins from the colon.

BLACKBERRY SOYA SMOOTHIE

139 calories

Ingredients

HEALING →

- 75g/3oz fresh blackberries
- 200ml/7floz unsweetened soya milk
- A pinch of ground cinnamon
- 1 tsp honey
- Water

Method

1 Rinse the blackberries and place them in the NUTRiBULLET tall cup.

2 Add the cinnamon, honey and soya milk. Make sure the ingredients do not go past the MAX line on your machine.

3 Add a little water if needed to take it up to the MAX line.

4 Twist on the NUTRiBULLET blade and blend until smooth.

CHEF'S NOTE
Blackberries are rich in antioxidants, have anti-bacterial properties and help in cleansing the blood. If eaten regularly, they may even help to delay the ageing process.

COCONUT BERRY BLAST

373 calories

Ingredients

CLEANSING

- 150g/5oz mixed berries (blueberries, raspberries or blackberries)
- 100ml/3½floz light coconut milk
- 25ml/1floz coconut water
- 15g/½oz rolled oats
- Water

Method

1 Rinse the berries well.

2 Add all the ingredients to the NUTRiBULLET tall cup. Make sure the ingredients do not go past the MAX line on your machine.

3 Add a little more water if needed to take it up to the MAX line.

4 Twist on the NUTRiBULLET blade and blend until smooth.

CHEF'S NOTE
Berries are great for cleansing due to the antioxidant and fibre content: exactly what you need to purge toxins and replenish your body.

BLACKCURRANT YOGHURT SMOOTHIE

258 calories

Ingredients

- 100g/4oz blackcurrants
- 1 small banana
- 150g/5oz apple
- 200ml/7floz apple juice
- 1 tbsp natural yoghurt
- Water

Method

1 Rinse the blackcurrants.

2 Peel the banana and break into three pieces. Core the apple.

3 Add everything to the NUTRiBULLET tall cup. Make sure the ingredients do not go past the MAX line on your machine.

4 Add a little water if needed to take it up to the MAX line.

5 Twist on the NUTRiBULLET blade and blend until smooth.

CHEF'S NOTE

Eaten regularly, blackcurrants are believed to brighten the complexion, and cleanse the skin. They have also been used to treat dark spots and skin diseases.

FRUIT & GINGER SMOOTHIE

306 calories

Ingredients

- 200g/7oz orange
- 2cm/1 inch fresh peeled ginger
- 1 tbsp honey
- 2 tbsp low fat yoghurt

- 1 small banana
- 1 tbsp lemon juice
- Water

Method

1 Peel and de-seed the orange.

2 Finely grate the ginger.

3 Peel the banana and break into three pieces.

4 Add everything to the tall cup. Make sure the ingredients do not go past the MAX line on your machine.

5 Add a little water if needed to take it up to the MAX line.

6 Twist on the NUTRiBULLET blade and blend until smooth.

CHEF'S NOTE

The healing and detoxifying properties of ginger may be due to its high levels of gingerol and shoga, which are anti-inflammatory.

RUBY JUICE

215 calories

Ingredients

HEART HEALTHY

- 150g/5oz beetroot
- 200g/7oz apple
- 140g/4½oz grapefruit
- Water

Method

1 Peel the beetroot.

2 Rinse and core the apple.

3 Peel and de-seed the grapefruit.

4 Add everything to the NUTRiBULLET tall cup. Top up with ice cubes and water.

5 Make sure the ingredients do not go past the MAX line on your machine.

6 Twist on the NUTRiBULLET blade and blend until smooth.

CHEF'S NOTE

Grapefruit contains natural acids that cleanse the skin as well as vitamin C which acts as an antioxidant. It is also high in potassium which supports cellular cleansing and helps tone the skin.

ALMOND CLEANSE

325 calories

Ingredients

- 1 tbsp ground almonds
- 100g/3½oz apple
- 1 small banana
- 2 tbsp low fat yoghurt
- 200ml/7floz unsweetened almond milk
- ½ tsp ground cinnamon
- Water

Method

1 Rinse and core the apple.

2 Peel the banana and break into three pieces.

3 Add all the ingredients to the NUTRiBULLET tall cup. Make sure they do not go past the MAX line on your machine.

4 Add a little water if needed to take it up to the MAX line.

5 Twist on the NUTRiBULLET blade and blend until smooth.

CHEF'S NOTE
Almonds contain antioxidants which cleanse toxins.

Skinny
NUTRiBULLET
DETOX SMOOTHIES

RASPBERRY, CHERRY & GINGER DETOX

SERVES 1

292 calories

Ingredients

- 125g/4oz raspberries
- 175ml/6floz unsweetened almond milk
- 50g/2oz pitted cherries
- 1½ tbsp honey
- 2 tsp finely grated root ginger
- 1 tsp ground flaxseed
- 2 tsp lemon juice
- Ice
- Water

Method

1 Wash the raspberries well and make sure all the cherries have been pitted.

2 Place all the ingredients in the NUTRiBULLET tall cup, finishing with ice.

3 Make sure the ingredients do not go past the MAX line on your machine.

4 Add a little water if needed to take it up to the MAX line.

5 Twist on the NUTRiBULLET blade and blend until smooth.

CHEF'S NOTE
Cherries contain natural aspirin that helps with inflammation and pectin, which helps to flush out cholesterol and synthetic chemicals from food additives.

28

SPICED SPINACH SMOOTHIE

83 calories

Ingredients

NATURALLY SWEET ➜

- 2cm/1 inch piece root ginger
- 1 tsp ground cinnamon
- 225g/8oz spinach
- 1 tsp agave nectar
- Water

Method

1 Rinse the spinach and cherries well. Peel & grate the ginger.

2 Add everything to the NUTRiBULLET tall cup, making sure the ingredients do not go past the MAX line on your machine.

3 Twist on the NUTRiBULLET blade and blend until smooth.

CHEF'S NOTE
Raw spinach contains far more cleansing nutrients than cooked spinach.

BEETROOT BURST

135 calories

Ingredients

ANTIOXIDANT +

- 150g/5oz orange
- 50g/2oz beetroot
- 100ml/3½floz pomegranate juice
- Ice cubes

Method

1 Peel the beetroot and orange. Deseed the orange and place both in the NUTRiBULLET tall cup.

2 Pour in the pomegranate juice. Make sure the ingredients do not go past the MAX line on your machine.

3 Add ice, twist on the NUTRiBULLET blade and blend until smooth.

CHEF'S NOTE
Beetroot helps detoxify the liver and therefore has a generally cleansing effect on your body's other systems.

HERB DETOX JUICE

160 calories

Ingredients

- 50g/2oz kale
- 100g/3½oz mango
- 1 stalk celery
- 125g/4oz orange

- 1 tbsp chopped flat-leaf parsley
- 1 tbsp chopped fresh mint
- Water

Method

1 Rinse the kale, celery. Cut the thick stems from the kale and roughly chop.

2 Peel and de-stone the mango.

3 Add all the ingredients to the NUTRiBULLET tall cup. Make sure they do not go past the MAX line on your machine.

4 Add a little water if needed to take it up to the MAX line.

5 Twist on the NUTRiBULLET blade and blend until smooth.

CHEF'S NOTE
Celery and parsley are both diuretics that help flush toxins from your body.

CHOCOLATE STRAWBERRY MILK

311 calories

Ingredients

FLAVENOIDS +

- 1 tbsp dark cocoa powder
- 120ml/4floz light coconut milk
- 100g/3½oz strawberries
- Ice

Method

1 Rinse the strawberries and remove the green tops.

2 Place them in the NUTRiBULLET tall cup, together with the coconut milk and cocoa powder. Add ice, but make sure it doesn't go past the MAX line on your machine.

3 Twist on the NUTRiBULLET blade and blend until smooth.

CHEF'S NOTE
Dark cocoa contains antioxidants that regular cocoa doesn't have.

SPINACH, PEAR & GRAPE SMOOTHIE

275 calories

Ingredients

- 60g/2½oz spinach
- 100g/3½oz pear
- 15 seedless grapes

- 4 tbsp low fat Greek yoghurt
- 30g/1oz chopped avocado
- 1 tbsp fresh lime juice

Method

1 Rinse the spinach, pear and grapes. Core the pear, but don't peel it. Peel and de-stone the avocado

2 Add everything to the NUTRiBULLET tall cup. Make sure the ingredients do not go past the MAX line on your machine.

3 Add a little water if needed to take it up to the MAX line.

4 Twist on the NUTRiBULLET blade and blend until smooth.

CHEF'S NOTE

Grapes have natural antioxidants called phytochemicals. The seeds contain flavonoids that are also thought to help strengthen blood vessels and improve circulation.

CORIANDER GINGER SMOOTHIE

234 calories

Ingredients

- 75g/3oz pear
- 40g/1½oz avocado
- 150g/5oz cucumber
- 2 tsp lemon juice
- 1 tbsp coriander leaves
- 75g/3oz kale
- 1cm/½ inch fresh root ginger
- 120ml/4floz coconut water
- 1 tbsp pumpkin seeds
- Water

Method

1 Rinse the pear, cucumber, coriander and kale. Remove any thick stalks from the kale. Core and roughly chop the pear. Chop the cucumber. Peel and grate the ginger.

2 Add everything to the NUTRiBULLET tall cup. Make sure the ingredients do not go past the MAX line on your machine.

3 Add a little water if needed to take it up to the MAX line.

4 Twist on the NUTRiBULLET blade and blend until smooth.

CHEF'S NOTE
Coriander helps to build healthy skin and hair, and is thought to potentially reduce the risk of heart disease and diabetes.

FRUIT FLAX JUICE

271 calories

Ingredients

FIBRE FLAX

- 1 tbsp flax seeds
- 125g/4oz raspberries
- 40g/1½oz blueberries
- 60g/2½oz orange
- 1 scoop vanilla protein powder

Method

1 Rinse the raspberries and blueberries. Peel the orange, deseed and break into rough segments.

2 Add everything to the NUTRiBULLET tall cup, finishing with ice. Make sure the ice does not go past the MAX line on your machine.

3 Twist on the NUTRiBULLET blade and blend until smooth.

CHEF'S NOTE

Flax seeds contain vitamins, minerals, omega-3 fatty acids and fibre. They can help eliminate toxins from the body, regulate the metabolism and reduce blood sugar level.

PROTEIN PEACH & GREEN TEA DETOX

159 calories

Ingredients

PROTEIN+

- 1 scoop soy protein powder, vanilla flavour
- 250ml/8½floz green tea
- 75g/3oz peach
- Ice cubes

Method

1 Wash, halve and de-stone the peach.

2 Make sure the green tea is cooled to room temperature and add everything to the NUTRiBULLET tall cup.

3 Make sure the ingredients do not go past the MAX line on your machine.

4 Twist on the NUTRiBULLET blade and blend until smooth.

CHEF'S NOTE
Peaches are said to help calm an upset stomach and detox the kidneys and bladder.

DARK DETOX

279
calories

Ingredients

- ½ small banana
- 50g/2oz blueberries
- 40g/1½oz avocado
- 120ml/4floz unsweetened almond milk

- 1 tsp spirulina
- 1 tbsp pumpkin seeds
- Water

Method

1 Rinse the berries.

2 Peel the banana and the avocado. De-stone the avocado.

3 Add all the ingredients apart from water to the NUTRiBULLET tall cup. Make sure the ingredients do not go past the MAX line on your machine.

4 Add a little water if needed to take it up to the MAX line.

5 Twist on the NUTRiBULLET blade and blend until smooth.

CHEF'S NOTE
Spirulina is a form of blue-green algae with powerful healing and cleansing properties.

BLUEBERRY COCONUT MILK

310 calories

Ingredients

- 100g/3½oz blueberries
- 300ml/10½floz light coconut milk
- A pinch of ground cinnamon
- 1 tsp honey
- 1 tbsp chia seeds
- Water

Method

1 Rinse the blueberries. Add them to the NUTRiBULLET tall cup, along with the other ingredients, making sure not go past the MAX line on your machine.

2 Add a little water if needed to take it up to the MAX line.

3 Twist on the NUTRiBULLET blade and blend until smooth.

CHEF'S NOTE
Chia seeds contain high amounts of both soluble and insoluble fibre, and help to clean out the digestive tract.

GREEN ALMOND MILK

333 calories

Ingredients

- 40g/1½oz pear
- 40g/1½oz avocado
- 225g/8oz spinach
- 60ml/2floz coconut water
- 250ml/8½floz unsweetened almond milk
- 1 tsp chia seeds
- 1 tbsp pumpkin seeds
- Water

Method

1 Wash the spinach and the pear. Core the pear but don't peel it.

2 Peel and de-stone the avocado.

3 Add all the ingredients except water to the NUTRiBULLET tall cup. Make sure they do not go past the MAX line on your machine.

4 Add a little water if needed to take it up to the MAX line.

5 Twist on the NUTRiBULLET blade and blend until smooth.

CHEF'S NOTE
One teaspoon of chia seeds holds almost 2 grams of fibre, excellent for flushing out the system.

APPLE & SPICED SPINACH ICE CRUSH

231 calories

Ingredients

VITAMIN C+

- 250ml/8½floz freshly squeezed orange juice
- 150g/5oz apple
- 2 tsp grated fresh ginger
- 125g/4oz spinach
- Ice cubes

Method

1 Rinse the apple and the spinach. Core and chop the apple but don't peel it.

2 Add all the ingredients to the NUTRiBULLET tall cup, finishing with ice cubes to taste. Make sure the ingredients do not go past the MAX line on your machine.

3 Twist on the NUTRiBULLET blade and blend until smooth.

CHEF'S NOTE
High in antioxidants, nutrients and vitamin C, fresh orange juice is a great detox ingredient.

CREAMY ALMOND, MANGO & BANANA

304 calories

Ingredients

- 100g/3½oz mango
- ½ small banana
- 125ml/4floz unsweetened almond milk
- 75ml/2½floz fresh orange juice
- 2 tbsp low fat natural yoghurt
- 1 tsp lime juice
- 5 raw almonds
- 1 tsp grated fresh ginger

Method

1 Peel, stone and cube the mango.

2 Peel the banana.

3 Add everything to the NUTRiBULLET tall cup. Make sure the ingredients do not go past the MAX line on your machine.

4 Twist on the NUTRiBULLET blade and blend until smooth.

CHEF'S NOTE

Bananas are rich in fibre, vitamins B6, and minerals like potassium and manganese, which make them very nutritious and great for detox.

FIG & GRAPE SMOOTHIE

112 calories

Ingredients

- 2 figs
- 50g/2oz red, seedless grapes
- 75g/3oz baby spinach
- Pinch of ground cinnamon
- Water
- Ice cubes

Method

1 Rinse the grapes & the spinach and place in the NUTRiBULLET tall cup.

2 Scoop out the pink flesh from the figs, and add.

3 Add the cinnamon and water. Top with ice cubes making sure not to pass the MAX line on your machine.

4 Twist on the NUTRiBULLET blade and blend until smooth.

CHEF'S NOTE

Figs are high in antioxidants and fibre, helping the body overcome damaging foods.

Skinny

NUTRiBULLET

SUPERFOOD SMOOTHIES

SWEET GOJI SMOOTHIE

196 calories

Ingredients

- 1 tbsp dried goji berries
- 50g/2oz strawberries
- 1 tsp honey
- 250ml/8½floz unsweetened almond milk
- Water
- Ice

Method

1 Soak the goji berries in a little water for around 15 minutes.

2 Rinse the strawberries well and remove the green tops.

3 Place all the berries in the NUTRiBULLET tall cup. Add the honey, almond milk and ice to taste, making sure the ingredients do not go past the MAX line on your machine.

4 Top up with a little water if needed.

5 Twist on the NUTRiBULLET blade and blend until smooth.

CHEF'S NOTE
Goji berries are a wonderful superfood - they're packed with antioxidants, vitamins, minerals and fibre.

AVOCADO, BLUEBERRY & CHIA SMOOTHIE

297 calories

Ingredients

- 75g/3oz avocado
- 50g/2oz fresh blueberries
- 1 tbsp chia seeds
- ¼ tsp cinnamon
- 2 tsp honey
- Water

Method

1 Rinse the blueberries well and place in the NUTRiBULLET tall cup.

2 Peel and de-stone the avocado.

3 Add the chia seeds, cinnamon and honey.

4 Add water to the MAX line on your machine.

5 Twist on the NUTRiBULLET blade and blend until smooth.

CHEF'S NOTE
Chia seeds are fabulously rich in omega 3, protein and antidioxidants.

KALE, COCONUT & PINEAPPLE SMOOTHIE

220 calories

Ingredients

- 140g/4½oz kale
- 175ml/6floz coconut water
- 1 small banana
- 2 tbsp low fat natural yogurt
- 50g/2oz pineapple
- 2 tsp honey
- Water

Method

1 Rinse the kale well and remove any thick stalks.

2 Peel the banana and break into three pieces. Peel the pineapple.

3 Add all the ingredients the to the NUTRiBULLET tall cup. Make sure they do not go past the MAX line on your machine.

4 Add a little water if needed to take it up to the MAX line.

5 Twist on the NUTRiBULLET blade and blend until smooth.

CHEF'S NOTE
Kale is believed to help prevent cardiovascular disease, several types of cancer, asthma, rheumatoid arthritis, and premature ageing of the skin.

GREEN TEA & MANGO SMOOTHIE

290 calories

Ingredients

- 250ml/8½floz green tea
- 150g/5oz mango
- 75g/3oz avocado

- 225g/8oz spinach
- A pinch of sea salt
- 1 tsp honey

Method

1 Make sure the green tea is no warmer than room temp.

2 Rinse the spinach well. Peel and de-stone the mango & avocado

3 Add all the ingredients to the NUTRiBULLET tall cup. Make sure they don't go past the MAX line on your machine.

4 Twist on the NUTRiBULLET blade and blend until smooth.

CHEF'S NOTE
The many nutrients found in avocados are thought to help protect your body from heart disease, cancer and degenerative eye disease.

MIGHTY BLUEBERRY FLAX SMOOTHIE

209 calories

Ingredients

- 125g/4oz blueberries
- 1 tbsp flax seeds
- 225g/8oz spinach
- 2 tbsp low fat Greek yogurt
- 100ml/3½floz coconut water
- Water

Method

1 Wash the spinach and blueberries well and place them in the NUTRiBULLET tall cup.

2 Add the flax seeds, yoghurt and coconut water. Make sure they don't go past the MAX line on your machine.

3 Top up with water as far as the MAX line.

4 Twist on the NUTRiBULLET blade and blend until smooth.

CHEF'S NOTE
Among many health benefits, flax seeds are believed to help lower blood pressure. They're also very rich in protein and fibre.

FRUIT CHIA SPICE SMOOTHIE

290 calories

Ingredients

- 50g/2oz blueberries
- 6 tbsp low fat Greek yogurt
- 1 tbsp chia seeds

- ½ tsp ground cinnamon
- 2 tsp honey
- Water

Method

1 Rinse the blueberries well. Add them to the NUTRiBULLET tall cup, along with the yoghurt, chia seeds, cinnamon and honey. Make sure they don't go past the MAX line on your machine.

2 Top up with water as far as the MAX line.

3 Twist on the NUTRiBULLET blade and blend until smooth.

CHEF'S NOTE
Cinnamon has been used throughout the ages to treat everything from a common cold to muscle spasms.

PEAR GREEN TEA

200 calories

Ingredients

- 175ml/6floz strong green tea, chilled
- Pinch cayenne pepper
- ½ lemon
- 2 tsp agave nectar
- 150g/5oz pear
- 2 tbsp low fat plain yogurt
- Ice cubes

Method

1 Rinse, core and quarter the pear, leaving the skin on.

2 Peel and deseed the lemon.

3 Add all the ingredients except the ice to the NUTRiBULLET tall cup. Add the ice, only as far as the MAX line on your machine.

4 Twist on the NUTRiBULLET blade and blend until smooth.

CHEF'S NOTE
Green tea is packed full of antioxidants to help fight against cancer, anxiety and fat. It's also good for heart and brain health and promotes oral hygiene.

ZIPPY BERRY & BANANA SMOOTHIE

251 calories

Ingredients

- 100g/3½oz mixed berries
- ½ small banana
- 225g/8oz spinach
- 1 tbsp coconut oil
- ¼ tsp cayenne pepper (or more to suit your own taste)
- Water

Method

1 Wash the berries and the spinach well. Add them to the NUTRiBULLET tall cup.

2 Peel banana and add to the cup along with the coconut oil and cayenne pepper.

3 Fill to the MAX line with water.

4 Twist on the NUTRiBULLET blade and blend until smooth.

CHEF'S NOTE

Spinach is a superfood well known for its nutrients and health benefits to bones, eyes & digestion. It's also extremely good for the complexion!

CHERRY BERRY HEMP BLEND

357 calories

Ingredients

- 1 small banana
- 125g/4oz cherries, pitted
- 120ml/4floz unsweetened almond milk
- 50g/2oz raspberries
- 1 tbsp hemp seeds
- Water

Method

1 Rinse the cherries and berries.

2 Place the pitted cherries in the NUTRiBULLET tall cup. Peel the banana, break it into 3 pieces and add.

3 Add the hemp seeds and almond milk making sure the ingredients do not go past the MAX line on your machine.

4 Top up with a little water if you like. Twist on the NUTRiBULLET blade and blend until smooth.

CHEF'S NOTE

Hemp seeds have a great mixture of omega 3 and omega 6 fatty acids, most important for overall health. They also contain all 20 amino acids, including the essential ones that our bodies can't produce alone

CACAO SUPERFOOD SMOOTHIE

319 calories

Ingredients

- 250ml/8½floz coconut water
- 50g/2oz avocado
- 50g/2oz raspberries
- 1 tbsp cacao powder
- ½ tsp vanilla extract
- 225g/8oz spinach

Method

1 Rinse the raspberries and spinach well.

2 Peel and de-stone the avocado.

3 Add all the ingredients to the NUTRiBULLET tall cup. Make sure they don't go past the MAX line on your machine.

4 Twist on the NUTRiBULLET blade and blend until smooth.

CHEF'S NOTE
Raw cacao contains nearly four times the antioxidant content of processed dark chocolate.

KALE & CRANBERRY BLAST

292 *calories*

Ingredients

- 225g/8oz fresh kale
- 100g/3½oz fresh cranberries
- 140g/4½oz orange

- 1 small banana
- 1 tbsp lime juice
- Water

Method

1 Rinse the kale and cranberries. Remove any thick stalks from the kale.

2 Peel and deseed the orange. Peel the banana and break into three.

3 Add all the ingredients to the NUTRiBULLET tall cup and top up with water to the MAX line on your machine.

4 Twist on the NUTRiBULLET blade and blend until smooth.

CHEF'S NOTE

Cranberries help prevent infections due to their high concentration of proanthocyanidins. They're also high in fibre, vitamin C and manganese.

GOJI & CACAO SMOOTHIE

340 calories

····· *Ingredients* ·····

- 250ml/8½floz coconut water
- 40g/1½oz avocado
- 3 tbsp low fat natural yogurt
- 100g/3½oz strawberries
- 1 tbsp goji berries

- 1 tbsp cacao powder
- ¼ tsp cinnamon
- A pinch of sea salt
- 1 tsp coconut oil
- Water

····· *Method* ·····

1 Rinse the strawberries and remove the green tops.

2 Add all the ingredients to the NUTRiBULLET tall cup. Make sure they don't go past the MAX line on your machine.

3 Twist on the NUTRiBULLET blade and blend until smooth.

CHEF'S NOTE

Goji berries have higher levels of antioxidants than nearly all other superfoods – except cacao!

WATERMELON & ACAI SMOOTHIE

250 calories

Ingredients

- 375g/13oz watermelon
- 1 tbsp acai powder
- 1 tbsp chia seeds
- 1 tbsp lemon juice
- 1 tsp agave nectar
- Water
- Ice

Method

1 Scoop out the watermelon flesh, deseed and place in the NUTRiBULLET tall cup.

2 Add all the other ingredients, finishing with ice as far as the MAX line on your machine.

3 Twist on the NUTRiBULLET blade and blend until smooth.

CHEF'S NOTE
Watermelon is believed to have the most potent cancer-fighting properties of any fruit.

LIGHT & BRIGHT GREEN JUICE

164 calories

Ingredients

- 225g/8oz spinach
- 75g/3oz cucumber
- 50g/2oz apple
- 1 tbsp chia seeds
- 1 tbsp lemon juice
- Water

Method

1 Rinse the spinach, cucumber and apple. Core the apple, don't peel.

2 Add the ingredients to the NUTRiBULLET tall cup, finishing with water to taste. Make sure not to pass the MAX line on your machine.

3 Twist on the NUTRiBULLET blade and blend until smooth.

CHEF'S NOTE

Chia seeds are high in omega-3 and particularly good for heart and bowel health.

CITRUS & COCONUT BURST

148 calories

Ingredients

- 120ml/4floz coconut water
- 175g/6oz grapefruit
- 2 sprigs fresh mint
- 2 tbsp goji berries
- 1 tsp agave nectar
- Ice

Method

1 Peel and deseed the grapefruit. Rinse the mint.

2 Add everything to the NUTRiBULLET tall cup, finishing with ice. Make sure the ingredients do not go past the MAX line on your machine.

3 Twist on the NUTRiBULLET blade and blend until smooth.

CHEF'S NOTE

Coconut water is packed with potassium, electrolytes and vitamin C.

Skinny

NUTRiBULLET

VEGETABLE SMOOTHIES

COCONUT SPINACH SMOOTHIE

340 calories

Ingredients

- 225g/8oz spinach
- 50g/2oz oats
- 1 tsp vanilla extract
- Pinch sea salt

- 120ml/4floz light coconut milk
- Water
- Ice cubes

Method

1 Rinse the spinach well and place in the NUTRiBULLET tall cup.

2 Add the coconut milk, oats, vanilla and salt and a few ice cubes to taste. Make sure the ingredients do not go past the MAX line on your machine.

3 Add water if needed to take it up to the MAX line.

4 Twist on the NUTRiBULLET blade and blend until smooth.

CHEF'S NOTE
Make sure you use light coconut milk not the full fat version.

CARROT & KALE SMOOTHIE

279 calories

Ingredients

NUTRIENT RICH →

- 300ml/10½floz carrots
- 75g/3oz kale
- 100g/3½oz avocado
- Water

Method

1 Rinse the kale and carrot well. Remove any thick stalks from the kale.

2 Peel and stone the avocado.

3 Nip the ends of the carrots and place all the ingredients in the NUTRiBULLET tall cup, making sure they do not go past the MAX line on your machine.

4 Add a little water if needed to take it up to the MAX line.

5 Twist on the NUTRiBULLET blade and blend until smooth.

CHEF'S NOTE
Carrots are rich in vitamin A, Vitamin C, Vitamin K, vitamin B8, pantothenic acid, folate, potassium, iron, copper and manganese.

CARROT & COCONUT SMOOTHIE

205 calories

Ingredients

VITAMIN B + ➔

- 75g/3oz carrot
- 50g/2oz avocado
- 225g/8oz spinach
- 120ml/4floz coconut water
- Ice cubes

Method

1 Rinse the spinach and carrot well.

2 Peel and stone the avocado.

3 Nip the ends of the carrots and place all the ingredients in the NUTRiBULLET tall cup, making sure they do not go past the MAX line on your machine.

4 Add the coconut water and ice. Make sure the ingredients do not go past the MAX line on your machine.

5 Twist on the NUTRiBULLET blade and blend until smooth.

CHEF'S NOTE

Coconut water is a natural isotonic drink that provides many of the same benefits as formulated sports drinks, including calcium, magnesium, phosphorus, sodium and potassium.

SPICED GREEN SMOOTHIE

119 calories

Ingredients

- 75g/3oz kale
- 2 celery stalks
- ½ tsp spirulina
- 1 pinch ground cinnamon
- 1 pinch ground ginger
- 100ml/3½oz light coconut milk
- Water

Method

1 Rinse the kale and the celery. Chop the celery and remove the thick stems from the kale. Add to the NUTRiBULLET tall cup.

2 Add the spirulina, cinnamon, ginger and coconut milk. Fill with water to the MAX line on your machine.

3 Twist on the NUTRiBULLET blade and blend until smooth.

CHEF'S NOTE

Spirulina is a great source of nutrients including vitamins B, C, D, A and E.

HEMP & SWEET PEPPER JUICE

115 calories

Ingredients

- 225g/8oz spinach
- 60g/2oz sweet yellow or orange pepper
- 1 stalk celery
- 1 tbsp hemp seeds
- 2 ice cubes
- Water

Method

1 Rinse the spinach, pepper and celery. Deseed the pepper. Roughly chop the celery.

2 Add the vegetable to the NUTRiBULLET tall cup. Add the hemp seeds and a couple of ice cubes. Make sure the ingredients do not go past the MAX line on your machine.

3 Top up with water if needed, as far as the MAX line.

4 Twist on the NUTRiBULLET blade and blend until smooth.

CHEF'S NOTE
For a sweeter tasting drink add a little agave nectar.

NUTTY CUCUMBER & DILL BLEND

250 calories

Ingredients

- 5 sprigs fresh dill
- 300g/11oz cucumber
- 2 tbsp lemon juice

- 10 raw pistachio nuts
- Water
- Ice cubes

Method

1 Rinse the dill and cucumber. Roughly chop the cucumber. Shell the pistachios and add these all to the NUTRiBULLET tall cup.

2 Add the lemon juice, and a few ice cubes. Make sure the ingredients do not go past the MAX line on your machine.

3 Top up with a little water to take it up to the MAX line.

4 Twist on the NUTRiBULLET blade and blend until smooth.

CHEF'S NOTE
Pistachios are a good source of fibre, protein, and heart-healthy fats.

HEARTY VEGETABLE SMOOTHIE

237 calories

Ingredients

- 250ml/8½floz unsweetened almond milk
- 225g/8oz spinach
- 175g/6oz tomatoes
- 150g/5oz courgette
- Pinch sea salt
- Pinch cayenne pepper
- Water

Method

1 Rinse the spinach, tomatoes & courgettes and roughly chop.

2 Add the vegetables and almond milk to the NUTRiBULLET tall cup. Add the salt and Cayenne pepper. Make sure the ingredients do not go past the MAX line on your machine.

3 Add a little water if needed to take it up to the MAX line.

4 Twist on the NUTRiBULLET blade and blend until smooth.

CHEF'S NOTE
Nutribullet Tip....if you sometimes find your ingredients won't all fit in your cup under the max line. Try blending some together first to make room for the other ingredients.

RED DEVIL

263 calories

Ingredients

- 200g/7oz tomato
- 60g/2oz red pepper
- 75g/3oz lettuce
- 100g/3½oz avocado
- ½ tsp ground cinnamon
- Water

Method

1 Rinse the tomato, pepper and lettuce. Core and roughly chop the pepper.

2 Peel and de-stone the avocado.

3 Add everything to the NUTRiBULLET tall cup. Make sure the ingredients do not go past the MAX line on your machine.

4 Add a little water if needed to take it up to the MAX line.

5 Twist on the NUTRiBULLET blade and blend until smooth.

CHEF'S NOTE
Tomatoes are an excellent source of vitamin C and other antioxidants.

CUCUMBER COCONUT BLEND

309 calories

Ingredients

- 150g/5oz cucumber
- 1 tbsp fresh flat leaf parsley
- 225g/8oz spinach
- ½ lemon
- 100g/3½oz avocado,
- 250ml/8½floz coconut water
- Ice cubes

Method

1 Rinse the cucumber, parsley and spinach. Roughly chop the cucumber. Peel and de-stone the avocado. Peel and deseed lemon.

2 Add all the ingredients to the NUTRiBULLET tall cup, finishing with ice to taste, but make sure you do not go past the MAX line on your machine.

3 Twist on the NUTRiBULLET blade and blend until smooth.

CHEF'S NOTE
Parsley is rich in many vital vitamins, including Vitamin C, B 12, K and A.

MEGA VEGGIE SPICE JUICE

255 calories

Ingredients

- 125g/4oz tomato
- 150g/5oz cucumber
- ½ clove garlic
- 1 stalk celery
- 150g/5oz romaine lettuce
- 100g/3½oz avocado
- ¼ tsp turmeric
- 1 tbsp lemon juice
- 1 tbsp chopped fresh mint leaves
- 1 tsp ground ginger
- 1 pinch cayenne pepper
- Ice

Method

1 Rinse the ingredients well. Roughly chop the cucumber, celery and lettuce.

2 Peel the garlic and avocado. De-stone the avocado.

3 Add everything to the NUTRiBULLET tall cup, finishing with ice. Make sure the ingredients do not go past the MAX line on your machine.

4 Twist on the NUTRiBULLET blade and blend until smooth.

CHEF'S NOTE
Ginger has a long history of use for relieving the symptoms of nausea, motion sickness and pain.

VEGGIE FLAX SMOOTHIE

392
calories

Ingredients

- 100g/3½oz avocado
- 150g/5oz cucumber
- 1 tbsp flax seeds
- 125g/4oz tomato

- 75g/3oz kale
- 1 tbsp lemon juice
- 250ml/8½floz unsweetened almond milk
- Water

Method

1 Rinse the kale and cucumber.

2 Peel and de-stone the avocado. Roughly chop the cucumber and remove the thick stalks from the kale

3 Put all the ingredients except water into the NUTRiBULLET tall cup. Make sure they do not go past the MAX line on your machine.

4 Add a little water if needed to take it up to the MAX line.

5 Twist on the NUTRiBULLET blade and blend until smooth.

CHEF'S NOTE
Flaxseeds are a rich source of micronutrients, dietary fibre, manganese, vitamin B1, and the essential fatty acid omega-3.

CREAMY ALMOND BUTTER SMOOTHIE

389 calories

Ingredients

- 75g/3oz cucumber
- 50g/2oz avocado
- 1 tbsp almond butter
- 1 tbsp flax seeds
- 2cm/1inch piece fresh root ginger
- 1 tsp ground cinnamon
- 225g/8oz spinach
- 200ml/7floz unsweetened almond milk
- Ice cubes

Method

1 Rinse the spinach & cucumber and roughly chop. Peel and de-stone the avocado.

2 Peel and grate the ginger.

3 Add all the ingredients to the NUTRiBULLET tall cup. Make sure they do not go past the MAX line on your machine.

4 Twist on the NUTRiBULLET blade and blend until smooth.

CHEF'S NOTE
Almond butter is a source of vitamin E, copper, magnesium, and high quality protein.

SUPER GREEN JUICE

279 calories

Ingredients

- 50g/2oz broccoli
- 75g/3oz kale
- 225g/8oz spinach
- 100g/3½oz avocado

- ½ lemon
- Water
- Ice cubes

Method

1 Wash the broccoli, kale and spinach. Cut any thick stems off the kale.

2 Peel and de-stone the avocado. Peel and deseed the lemon.

3 Place everything in the NUTRiBULLET tall cup and add some ice cubes . Make sure the ingredients do not go past the MAX line on your machine.

4 Add a little water if needed.

5 Twist on the NUTRiBULLET blade and blend until smooth.

CHEF'S NOTE
Broccoli contains high levels of vitamins A and D.

BLENDED CARROT CAKE

399 calories

Ingredients

- 100g/3½oz avocado
- 50g/2oz carrot
- 3 tbsp raisins
- 225g/8oz spinach
- 100ml/3½floz unsweetened almond milk
- 150ml/5floz coconut water
- ½ tsp cinnamon
- ½ tsp vanilla extract
- Water

Method

1 Wash the carrot and spinach. Nip the ends off the carrot.

2 Peel and de-stone the avocado.

3 Add everything except the coconut water to the NUTRiBULLET tall cup. Make sure the ingredients do not go past the MAX line on your machine.

4 Top up with water if needed to take it up to the MAX line.

5 Twist on the NUTRiBULLET blade and blend until smooth.

CHEF'S NOTE
Almond milk is low in fat and high in energy, proteins, lipids and fibre.

NUT BUTTER & SPINACH SMOOTHIE

396 calories

Ingredients

- 1 tbsp cashew butter
- 1 tbsp cashews
- 225g/8oz spinach
- 100g/3½oz avocado
- 250ml coconut water
- Ice cubes

Method

1 Rinse the spinach well. Peel and de-stone the avocado.

2 Add all the ingredients to the NUTRiBULLET tall cup, finishing with ice. Make sure they do not go past the MAX line on your machine.

3 Twist on the NUTRiBULLET blade and blend until smooth.

CHEF'S NOTE
Vary the nuts and nut butter to suit your own taste but be aware of the calorie count if you do this.

RED BEET JUICE

131 calories

Ingredients

RETENOIDS+

- 165g/5½oz fresh beetroot
- 75g/3oz red lettuce
- 250ml/8½floz coconut water
- Water

Method

1 Wash the lettuce. Peel the beetroot and add to the NUTRiBULLET tall cup.

2 Pour in the coconut water. Make sure the ingredients do not go past the MAX line on your machine.

3 Add a little water if needed to take it up to the MAX line.

4 Twist on the NUTRiBULLET blade and blend until smooth.

CHEF'S NOTE
Feel free to use raw or cooked beetroot for this simple light juice.

NUTTY GREEN CHIA SMOOTHIE

377 calories

Ingredients

- 225g/8oz spinach
- 100g/3½oz avocado
- 1 tbsp chopped fresh mint

- 2 tsp chia seeds
- 200ml/7floz unsweetened almond milk
- Water

Method

1 Rinse the spinach. Peel and de-stone the avocado.

2 Add everything to the NUTRiBULLET tall cup. Make sure the ingredients do not go past the MAX line on your machine.

3 Add a little water if needed to take it up to the MAX line.

4 Twist on the NUTRiBULLET blade and blend until smooth.

CHEF'S NOTE
Chia seeds can help raise HDL cholesterol – which is the good cholesterol that helps protect against heart attack and stroke.

Skinny

NUTRiBULLET

NATURALLY SWEET SMOOTHIES

COCOA AVOCADO SMOOTHIE

349 calories

Ingredients

- 75g/3oz avocado
- 1 small banana
- 30g/1oz raspberries
- 1 tbsp dark cocoa powder
- 200ml/7floz unsweetened almond milk
- Water

Method

1 Rinse the raspberries.

2 Peel and de-stone the avocado. Peel the banana and break into three pieces

3 Add everything to the NUTRiBULLET tall cup. Make sure the ingredients do not go past the MAX line on your machine.

4 Add a little water if needed to take it up to the MAX line.

5 Twist on the NUTRiBULLET blade and blend until smooth.

CHEF'S NOTE
You could also use soya milk as an alternative to almond milk.

SWEET GREEN SMOOTHIE

366 calories

Ingredients

- 1 small banana
- 150g/5oz seedless green grapes
- 4 tbsp low fat vanilla yoghurt
- 75g/3oz apple
- 50g/2oz fresh spinach
- Water

Method

1 Rinse the spinach, grapes and apple.

2 Core the apple and peel the banana.

3 Add all the ingredients to the NUTRiBULLET tall cup. Make sure they do not go past the MAX line on your machine.

4 Add a little water if needed to take it up to the MAX line.

5 Twist on the NUTRiBULLET blade and blend until smooth.

CHEF'S NOTE
Natural yoghurt instead of vanilla also works well.

SERVES 1

CREAMY DATE SMOOTHIE

372 calories

Ingredients

- ½ small banana
- 50g/2oz dates
- 40g/1½oz avocado

- 1 tsp almond butter
- 2 tsp cacao powder
- 200ml/7floz unsweetened almond milk

Method

1 Peel the banana. Halve and stone the dates.

2 Peel and de-stone the avocado.

3 Add everything to the NUTRiBULLET tall cup. Make sure the ingredients do not go past the MAX line on your machine.

4 Twist on the NUTRiBULLET blade and blend until smooth.

CHEF'S NOTE
Feel free to add more almond milk as far as the MAX line if you wish, but remember it will increase your calorie intake.

HONEY MANGO SMOOTHIE

256 calories

Ingredients

- 100g/3oz mango
- 4 tbsp natural low-fat yogurt
- 150ml/5floz unsweetened almond milk
- 1 tsp honey
- Pinch ground cardamom
- Water

Method

1 Peel and de-stone the mango.

2 Add to the NUTRiBULLET tall cup, along with the other ingredients.

3 Make sure the ingredients do not go past the MAX line on your machine.

4 Add a little water if needed to take it up to the MAX line.

5 Twist on the NUTRiBULLET blade and blend until smooth.

CHEF'S NOTE
Make sure your mango is ripe for maximum sweetness!

TROPICAL FRUIT MILK

214 calories

Ingredients

- 100g/3½oz mango
- ½ small banana
- 75ml/3floz light coconut milk
- 50g/2oz pineapple
- 60ml/2floz orange juice
- Water

Method

1 Peel and de-stone the mango.

2 Peel the banana and the pineapple.

3 Add everything to the NUTRiBULLET tall cup, making sure the ingredients do not go past the MAX line on your machine.

4 Add a little water if needed to take it up to the MAX line.

5 Twist on the NUTRiBULLET blade and blend until smooth.

CHEF'S NOTE
For extra creaminess, use a whole banana. Your smoothie will still be less than 300 calories.

PINEAPPLE SMOOTHIE

288 calories

Ingredients

MANGANESE +

- 400g/14oz fresh pineapple
- 1 small banana
- Ice cubes

Method

1 Peel the pineapple, cut it into chunks and drop into the NUTRiBULLET tall cup.

2 Peel the banana, break it into three pieces and add.

3 Add ice to taste, but make sure the ingredients do not go past the MAX line on your machine.

4 Twist on the NUTRiBULLET blade and blend until smooth.

CHEF'S NOTE
Pineapple contains a wealth of nutrients including potassium, copper & manganese.

RASPBERRY, BANANA & POMEGRANATE SMOOTHIE

169 calories

Ingredients

BLOOD CLEANSER

- 100g/3½oz raspberries
- 1 small banana
- 300ml/10½ floz pomegranate juice
- Water

Method

1 Rinse the raspberries.

2 Peel the banana and break into three pieces. Add them to the NUTRiBULLET tall cup.

3 Add the pomegranate juice, making sure the ingredients do not go past the MAX line on your machine.

4 Add a little water if needed to take it up to the MAX line.

5 Twist on the NUTRiBULLET blade and blend until smooth.

CHEF'S NOTE
Pomegranate is a great source of fibre.

FRUIT PUNCH

160 calories

Ingredients

- 100g/3½oz orange
- ½ kiwi fruit
- 1 small banana
- 50g/2oz pineapple
- Water
- Ice cubes

Method

1 Peel the kiwi fruit, banana & pineapple.

2 Peel & deseed the orange.

3 Add the fruit to the NUTRiBULLET tall cup

4 Add ice and water to taste, making make sure the ingredients do not go past the MAX line on your machine.

5 Twist on the NUTRiBULLET blade and blend until smooth.

CHEF'S NOTE
Pineapple is a good source of soluble fibre.

FRUITY PUMPKIN SEED SMOOTHIE

195 calories

Ingredients

MINERAL RICH

- 75g/3oz raspberries
- 4 tbsp low-fat natural yoghurt
- 1 tbsp honey
- 1 tbsp pumpkin seeds
- Water

Method

1 Rinse the raspberries. Add them to the NUTRiBULLET tall cup.

2 Add the yoghurt, honey & pumpkin seeds. Make sure the ingredients do not go past the MAX line on your machine.

3 Add a little water if needed to take it up to the MAX line.

4 Twist on the NUTRiBULLET blade and blend until smooth. Pour into a glass and sprinkle with the pumpkin seeds.

CHEF'S NOTE
Pumpkin seeds contain compounds known as phytosterols and free-radical scavenging antioxidants that can give your health an added boost.

PASSION SOYA SMOOTHIE

262 calories

Ingredients

LACTOSE FREE ➡️

- 100g/3½oz mango
- 100g/ 3½oz passion fruit
- 2 tbsp fat-free mango yogurt
- 120ml/4floz soya milk
- Water

Method

1 Peel, de-stone and cube the mango. Drop it in the NUTRiBULLET tall cup.

2 Halve the passion fruit and scoop out the flesh, adding it to the cup.

3 Add the other ingredients. Make sure they do not go past the MAX line on your machine.

4 Add a little water if needed to take it up to the MAX line.

5 Twist on the NUTRiBULLET blade and blend until smooth.

CHEF'S NOTE
Try with unsweetened almond milk instead of soya milk if you wish.

PROTEIN CHERRY BLAST

192 calories

Ingredients

AIDS SLEEP

- 125g/4oz cherries
- 1 scoop chocolate protein powder
- 250ml/8½ floz water

Method

1 Rinse and de-stone the cherries.

2 Mix the water and protein powder in the NUTRiBULLET tall cup. Add the cherries. Make sure the ingredients do not go past the MAX line on your machine.

3 Twist on the NUTRiBULLET blade and blend until smooth.

CHEF'S NOTE
Protein is vital to muscle growth and tissue repair.

FESTIVE PEAR & BANANA SHAKE

252 calories

Ingredients

- 175g/6oz pear
- ½ small banana
- 120ml/4floz semi-skimmed milk
- 2 tbsp low fat yoghurt

- 1 pinch ground cinnamon
- 1 pinch ground nutmeg

Method

1 Rinse, core and quarter the pear, leaving the skin on.

2 Peel the banana.

3 Add the fruit to the NUTRiBULLET tall cup followed by the other ingredients, making sure not to go past the MAX line on your machine.

4 Add a little water if needed to take it up to the MAX line.

5 Twist on the NUTRiBULLET blade and blend until smooth.

CHEF'S NOTE
As an alternative try using light coconut milk instead of semi-skimmed milk.

FRESH PEACH SOYA MILK

270 calories

Ingredients

FIBRE RICH

- 200g/7oz peach
- ½ small banana
- 200ml/7floz soya milk
- Ice

Method

1 Rinse, halve and de-stone the peaches leaving the skin on.

2 Peel the banana.

3 Add fruit to the NUTRiBULLET tall cup. Pour in the soya milk and add ice to taste. Make sure the ingredients do not go past the MAX line on your machine.

4 Twist on the NUTRiBULLET blade and blend until smooth.

CHEF'S NOTE
For a creamier finish use a combination of yoghurt and soya milk.

SERVES 1

ALMOND & CHIA PEACH SMOOTHIE

198 calories

Ingredients

- 1 small banana
- 125g/4oz peach
- 60g2½ oz strawberries

- 100ml/3½floz unsweetened almond milk
- 1 tbsp chia seeds
- Ice

Method

1 Rinse the peach and strawberries. Remove the green tops from the strawberries.

2 De-stone the peach but leave the skin on. Peel the banana and break into three pieces

3 Add the fruit and chia seeds to the NUTRiBULLET tall cup. Pour in the almond milk and add ice to taste. Make sure the ingredients do not go past the MAX line on your machine.

4 Twist on the NUTRiBULLET blade and blend until smooth.

CHEF'S NOTE
Chia seeds are an excellent source of omega-3 fatty acids.

MELON MILK

193 calories

Ingredients

CLEANSING →

- 200g/7oz honeydew melon
- 200ml/7½ floz unsweetened almond milk
- 1 tsp honey
- Ice

Method

1 Peel, deseed & roughly cube the melon. Place in the NUTRiBULLET tall cup.

2 Add the almond milk, honey and ice, making sure the ingredients do not go past the MAX line on your machine.

3 Twist on the NUTRiBULLET blade and blend until smooth.

CHEF'S NOTE
Try also with other types of melon, such as Galia and Cantaloupe.

SWEET CINNAMON BANANA MILK

340 calories

Ingredients

- 2 small bananas
- 3 tbsp low-fat vanilla yogurt
- 120ml/4floz skimmed milk
- 2 tsp honey
- Pinch of ground cinnamon
- Ice

Method

1 Peel the bananas and break each into three pieces.

2 Add everything to the NUTRiBULLET tall cup, finishing with ice. Make sure you don't go past the MAX line on your machine.

3 Twist on the NUTRiBULLET blade and blend until smooth.

CHEF'S NOTE
Experiment with more cinnamon for a warmer, spicier taste.

RASPBERRY & ORANGE ICE CRUSH

253 calories

Ingredients

FIGHTS AGEING

- 250g/9oz orange
- 125g/4oz raspberries
- 120ml/4floz low fat natural yoghurt
- Ice

Method

1 Rinse the raspberries well.

2 Peel & de-seed the orange.

3 Add everything to the NUTRiBULLET tall cup, making sure the ingredients do not go past the MAX line on your machine.

4 Twist on the NUTRiBULLET blade and blend until smooth.

CHEF'S NOTE
For extra sweetness add a teaspoon of agave nectar.

🍎 **CookNation**

Other
COOKNATION
TITLES

If you enjoyed 'The *Skinny* NUTRiBULLET Slimming Smoothies Recipe Book' you may also be interested in other '*Skinny*' NUTRiBULLET titles in the CookNation series.

Visit **www.bellmackenzie.com** to browse the full catalogue.

33766691R00055

Printed in Great Britain
by Amazon